IT'S

IN THE

A Play

VALERIE MASKELL

SAMUEL FRENCH

LONDON

NEW YORK TORONTO SYDNEY HOLLYWOOD

MADE AND PRINTED IN GREAT BRITAIN BY
LATIMER TREND & COMPANY LTD PLYMOUTH
MADE IN ENGLAND

CHARACTERS

Tracy
Nat, her husband
Lee, her neighbour
Kirk, Lee's husband
Dawn, Tracy's daughter
Rod, Tracy's son

The action takes place in the living-room of Nat's flat in a tower block

Time—A Saturday afternoon in the near future

IT'S ALL IN THE GAME

The living-room of a flat in a tower block. Afternoon

The scene is set on an open stage. The back wall only is required, and the entrance can be formed in this by the use of overlapping screens. The furniture consists of a very modern seating arrangement along this wall, and one or two cubes covered to match which may be sat on or used as occasional tables. In the centre of the back wall is a panel of switches, within easy reach of anyone sitting down. From this, Nat ostensibly controls light and sound. Above the panel is a huge blow-up of an aggressive, tousled young man in football gear. Near this, also displayed artistically on the wall, is a grubby red football shirt. On one of the cubes, downstage on a special stand, rests a shabby football. The wall and upholstery are cheerfully coloured and there are bright cushions

Tracy, a pretty woman, brightly and trimly dressed, enters. She carries a tray loaded with cans of beer, packets of crisps and cigarettes, which she proceeds to set on a table. As she does so she hums the "Match of the Day" tune. Having finished this, she turns to an imaginary television screen, about five feet by four, and proceeds to dust it. This screen is presumed to be set in the "fourth wall" facing the seating. (It is vital that this mime should be convincing and should create the size and position of the screen in the minds of the audience)

Lee (*off*) Tracy! Anyone at home?
Tracy Come in, love.

> *Lee enters; a bit younger and slimmer than Tracy, dressed in a somewhat similar style*

Lee You left the door on the latch again.
Tracy I'm always doing that.
Lee Well you shouldn't. It's not safe. You never know who might come wandering in.
Tracy I know. You did.

Lee But it might not be me next time. D'you want to get raped or something?

Tracy I'd be lucky.

Lee It's no laughing matter.

Tracy Well, what's the good of being serious? I tell Nat, one serious one's enough in the family.

Tracy is now satisfied with the state of the screen and sets out the contents of the tray on a table downstage

Lee Are you going to watch this afternoon?

Tracy Don't suppose I can get out of it.

Lee Trace, you're mad, you really are. The risks you take.

Tracy Where's the risk in not watching The Game? It's not compulsory, not yet, anyway.

Lee No, but if you were ever—well—in any trouble, it'd go against you that you aren't a watcher.

Tracy Well, I'm not going to get into any trouble, so stop worrying. There; beer, fags, crisps, lighter, ashtray, the lot.

Lee Clean shirt?

Tracy Yep. Ironed it this morning. Pure white cotton poplin. None of your drip-dries for Nat, not for The Game.

Lee Well, you don't spare any trouble, I'll say that. Where is he?

Tracy Having a shower. And Dawn's washing up. For once.

Lee Nice when we can use the machines again.

Tracy Still, they do take a lot of water. I suppose it's right really.

Lee I wouldn't put it past you to use yours anyway.

Tracy (*with a sharp glance*) Well, I don't.

Nat enters. He is a big cheerful man, about forty-five, wearing a white shirt and light trousers. His hair is damp from the shower

Nat Hallo, Lee. Why haven't you switched on, Trace? It's nearly Time. We've missed half the music.

Tracy There's five minutes yet.

Nat sits on the seat and manipulates the switches, watching the screen carefully

Nat You watching with us, Lee?

Lee No thanks. We always watch together. All four of us.

Nat As it should be. Best get along then. Come on, Tracy, take that apron off. You wouldn't like Bobby Setterfield to see you in that.

Tracy What's wrong with it?

Nat (*warningly*) Tracy! (*He turns up the sound*)

Martial music blares. Lee turns to go. Nat turns down the sound, speaking as Lee reaches the door

Hey, told her about Rod, have you?

Lee (*turning*) Yes, she told me yesterday. It's marvellous. No wonder you're proud. Third Under Secretary to the Minister for the Game!

Nat At twenty-three! Brilliant boy. Brilliant boy.

Tracy Don't know where he gets it from. All I know is, there wasn't much left over for Dawn.

Nat Dawn's a good girl, a very good girl. Never misses a Game. Where is she? Dawn! Time you were here!

Lee (*moving to the door*) And time I wasn't.

Dawn runs in, almost colliding with Lee: she is a leggy teenager, dressed in jeans and T-shirt, casual, but fresh and clean. She rushes to the seat and kneels up in front of the picture, spreading out her arms as though to embrace it

Dawn I love you, Bobby Setterfield. Win for us, Bobby. Win for us! (*She takes the ball off the stand and sits cuddling it*)

Nat Put that back.

Dawn Oh, Dad . . .

Nat Put it back I say.

Dawn does so. Nat pours himself a beer

Dawn (*to Lee*) Our Roddy's there. He's seeing The Game. Today.

Lee (*coming back into the room*) No! Is he?

Nat Yes, actually there, seeing it all.

Lee I've never met anyone who's actually been to a Game. What an experience.

Tracy Well, of course you've got to be pretty high up to get a ticket.

Nat Only Senior State Employees.

Dawn (*her eyes searching the screen*) Maybe we'll see him.

Tracy You'd have a job to pick anyone out of all those thousands.

Lee It's amazing to think they're all Senior State Employees.

Nat Or Ministers. My boy's there with all the Ministers.

Dawn P'raps he'll come and tell us about it afterwards.

Tracy He will if he can, I'm sure, but your brother's very busy, you know, very busy and important.

Dawn He could get from the Stadium in an hour. He's got a car.

Nat (*proudly*) Yes, allowed private transport now, that's another thing. Go where he likes, more or less.

Lee Gosh, I must get back. They're almost starting.

Nat, having poured out his beer, turns the sound up

  Lee goes out

Tracy sits down. Martial music and crowd noises come from the TV, followed by the voice of the Commentator. The Lights dim somewhat. Nat leans forward concentrating hard, becoming more and more worked up, finishing up kneeling in front of the screen. Dawn is even more uninhibited, jumping about, rolling on the floor and so on. (Ideally, the use of a Strobe light, which would show them in a succession of brief flashes would indicate the passage of time. If a Strobe is unobtainable a good effect can be obtained by bringing up rapidly changing lights of red, green and blue to suggest a reflection from the screen)

Commentator And it's US to kick off. We are in red shirts and black shorts while THEY are playing in a changed strip of all blue. And from the kick-off the ball is tapped back to Setterfield who tries to get Perkins away on the left wing but the ball goes straight into touch. The throw is taken by Philips a long one which finds Jordan and Jordan is brought down by Tiny Paterson. That really was a very hard tackle so early in the game and the referee is having a quiet word with Paterson. The free kick is taken by Jordan, a good one deep into the penalty area on to the head of Parker but he can't control it and it's over the line for a goal-kick to US . . .

After this his words are lost in crowd noises, screams from Dawn, etc. Groans and shouts of triumph from Nat, etc., until the Strobe or coloured light ceases and the normal light returns with the

*music and the Commentator's voice, indicating half-time. Nat turns
down the sound to a murmur. Dawn is lying on the floor*

Tracy (*matter of factly*) I'm going to make some tea. Up, Dawn
for goodness sake.

Dawn collapses on to the seat

Dawn (*murmuring*) Oh Bobby, oh Bobby.
Nat Did you see that? Did you see it? The way Bobby came
down, right through the lot of them.

Tracy goes out

Dawn Two-all. Two-all! Dad, what a game. Oh Bobby, you're
so wonderful!

Kirk rushes in

Kirk Did you see that? Did you see it? The way Bobby came
down . . .
Nat Right through the lot of them.
Kirk What a game.

Nat pours beer and hands one to Kirk

Nat Here you are, get that down you.
Kirk Need a beer after that. Thanks, pal.

They both drink thirstily

Kirk Thanks.
Tracy (*off*) D'you want some tea, Dawn?

Dawn is in a dream, cuddling and stroking the ball again

Tracy appears at the door

Tracy Dawn! D'you want some tea?

Tracy goes

Dawn Yes please, Mum. Oh, wasn't it marvellous.
Kirk What do you think of that new centre-forward, then?

Nat They've made a mistake there. No idea how to head a ball.

Kirk Not up to Phil Parry, never will be.

Nat Mind you, he could be nervous—he might improve.

Kirk But we need a win today, boy, as of today. If we don't get it . . .

Nat Production'll go down.

Kirk Marriages'll break up.

Nat Vandalism increase.

Kirk Suicides too.

Nat Absenteeism.

Kirk Robbery with violence.

Nat Battered wives.

Kirk We've got to have a win.

Nat Three weeks since the last one.

Kirk They've got a good team.

Nat A bloody good team.

Kirk They've got Tiny Paterson

Nat A million, they'd want for him.

Kirk Worth it though, worth it. If it rested with me . . .

Nat I'd say get him.

Kirk Get him.

Nat Get Tiny Paterson.

Kirk Even at a million.

Nat Production'd go up.

Kirk Vandalism'd go down.

Nat Everyone'd be smiling.

Kirk But we need a win today.

Nat I think we'll get it.

Kirk Think so?

Nat When we really need it, we get it.

Kirk I've noticed that.

Nat Brings out the best.

Tracy enters with a tea tray

Nat What about our Rod then, Trace? He's actually there, somewhere in that crowd, watching.

Tracy It's a great achievement.

Dawn He'll see Bobby Setterfield, actually see him. And Russ Parker.

Nat He'll see all the Players. In the flesh.
Kirk No wonder you're proud. Will he be coming home?
Tracy Not today. We can't expect him to come home today . . .
Dawn It's weeks since he came.
Nat He's got his own transport.
Tracy Well, we'll see. We mustn't expect too much.
Dawn He's very important.

The Commentator's voice, raised, is heard faintly

Kirk I'd better be getting back. Thanks for the beer. Cheerio.
Nat We'll make it today. You've got to have faith you know.
You've got to have faith in the team. (*He slaps Kirk on the
back and sees him to the exit*)

Kirk goes

*The ball is replaced on the stand. Tracy and Dawn settle down with
their tea. Nat lowers the lights and turns up the volume by means of
switches on the panel. Music, Commentator's voice and crowd
noises which start with enthusiasm and rise to a wild pitch of
excitement. Cries of triumph and groans of despair from the set,
and from Dawn and Nat. The Strobe light starts*

Commentator And I think we're about all set to begin. The
referee glances at his two watches, checks with his linesmen
and with a sharp blast on his whistle, gets play under way.
And immediately the ball is passed out to the right wing,
where Setterfield beats one man but can't get past the second
and the ball cannons off a defender for the throw-in. It's taken
quickly; Perkins crosses deep into the area but it's gathered
safely by the keeper who clears upfield . . .

*Nat falls to his knees, Dawn grabs the ball and Tracy leans forward
anxiously. After only two or three flashes the Strobe stops, the
sound stops and the Lights go up*

*Rod is standing with his hand on the switch panel. There is a
moment's astonished silence. Nat rises in extreme consternation*

Nat Rod, you've switched off. You've switched off The Game, old man. We were watching The Game. (*He rises and moves to the switch*)

Rod is a tall, well-built young man in dark quasi-uniform clothes

Rod Leave it, Dad.

Dawn rises

Dawn, I said leave it.

Tracy (*rising*) But the Game, Roddy. Your Dad must watch the Game.

Nat (*angrily*) What's the matter with you? You may be a State Employee, but——

Tracy Are you all right, dear, what's happened?

Dawn Turn it on, Roddy, turn it ON!

Nat But you can't stop us watching the Game.

Rod Shut up, all of you. There isn't any bloody Game!

A second's pause

Nat What in hell do you mean? Have you gone mad?

Nat switches on. The crowd roars momentarily and meaninglessly

Rod switches off. Dawn stretches out her hand to switch on again. Rod stops her

Tracy Leave it, Nat. Leave it, Dawn. Five minutes won't matter. Let Rod say what he wants to say, then you can go back to the Game.

Rod The Game, the Game. I tell you there isn't any Game.

Nat (*quietly, humouring him*) Now come on, son, come on. Sit down and tell us about it.

Rod sits

Dawn He's gone mad. He's schizophrenic. (*She sits on the floor*)

Tracy Shut up, Dawn. Now, Roddy, go on.

Rod It's all a con. A bloody great con. I had to come and tell you. I couldn't let you go on being fooled like the rest. (*He is profoundly disturbed, it is obvious he has come for comfort as much as anything else*) You knew I was going to the Game today. Well, we all left Government Complex in plenty of time, and got out to the Stadium. People lining the streets and cheering us as we went past. All the usual guff, checking passes, automatic doors, even though we were all Government. Then the barriers and no-one within three miles of the Stadium. Then we got there. Hell of a noise going on. Music, shouting— I was really excited. God, I was so excited. Then we went in. No-one there, stands empty, no crowd, no players. In the middle, a damn great computer, clicking away. Just that, nothing else. A damn great computer, and sound pouring from the amplifiers.

Nat But where is it, then? Where's the Game?

Rod Can't you understand? Oh, my God, can't you understand? THERE IS NO GAME! It doesn't exist. Hasn't done so for years and years—it's just a computer, linking up bits of video tape. It's all calculated. How often we win, how often we lose. so as to keep up morale, keep everyone happy and working, You'll never get to see a Game, Dad. Whatever miracles of production you achieve, however many tickets in the Great Ballot have your number on, because nobody does. It's always somebody else that wins, somebody you've never met, and never meet. Because it's all a great big con. There isn't any Game.

Nat (*baffled*) But the Ministry? The Ministry for the Game? You're part of that now. There must be a Game. What about the Ministry?

Rod That's what we do, that's our job, to trick the public—kid them along . . .

Tracy I'm not suprised. I've always thought . . . Well, I don't know.

Dawn Mum, does he mean there's no Bobby Setterfield?

Tracy Not now, love. But perhaps there was once.

Dawn Bobby, oh Bobby, how could you. (*She bursts into tears*)

Nat (*bewildered and angry*) It's rubbish. He's talking rubbish. It's like Dawn said, he's schizophrenic. Mad, gone mad. That's it. You've gone mad, son.

Tracy I don't think so, Nat. I think it's the truth.

Nat I don't get it. I don't get it at all. You mean, what we see, what we wait for, and hope for, and pay for, what we build our lives on, what keeps us going—isn't there?

Rod That's it, Dad. That's what I'm telling you.

Nat (*tiredly*) I've heard rumours, there's always rumours, but you don't take any notice of them. You've got to have faith in the

Game. I've always been a Watcher, brought up a Watcher;
you and Dawn watched the Game ever since you can re-
member. And now you come, YOU come—and tell me this!
My God I ought to throw you out. I ought to . . . (*He sits down
utterly broken and hopeless*)

Dawn cuddles the ball and weeps quietly

Tracy Why did you tell him, Rod. Why couldn't you leave well
alone?

Rod I couldn't let you two go on believing in a lie, I suppose. Or
—no—it wasn't that. You see most of the people I work with,
they've got there in their minds long before they get taken to
the Stadium. But I hadn't. I kept on thinking I'm going to see
the Game. At last! No wonder they laughed themselves sick. I
suppose I just—came home. Sorry, Mum.

Tracy Never mind, love. You'll get over it. And so will he, in a
different way.

Rod (*rising*) I'd better be getting along. They're not keen on us
seeing too much of our families.

Tracy But you'll come again soon?

Rod When I can. When I can. But I'll be pretty busy with this
new job.

Tracy Don't you want some tea before you go?

Rod No—no—I must get along. I'm sorry I upset Dad and
Dawn. You'll see they don't talk, won't you. If they found out
I'd told you . . .

Tracy They won't, I'll see to that. Off you go now.

Rod Good-bye, Mum.

*Rod looks at Nat who is staring into space, and at Dawn who is
still cuddling the ball, and weeping quietly. Then he goes*

*Nat takes the jersey down from the wall, looks at it, and lets it drop
on the floor*

Dawn Oh Bobby, why have you left me? I'd have done anything
for you.

Nat I can't take it, Trace, old girl. I feel I've lost everything.
Why couldn't I have died without finding out. For years and
years you go on doing your best, trying to be—worthy—of the
Team. Everything is for them—so that one day, maybe, you'll
get a ticket to go and see (*He breaks down*)

Tracy (*briskly after a pause*) Get up, Dawn. Put the ball back. Drink your tea. Here, you have some tea too, Nat, and start thinking sensibly.

Nat Sensibly!

Tracy (*pouring tea*) Look at the real facts. Ten minutes ago you were watching the Game. Nothing has changed since then.

Nat and Dawn Nothing changed?

Tracy Nothing at all. Except in your minds. All right, there's no Game. But there hasn't been a Game for years and years. Rod said so. It's what I've always thought, anyway. All the winning and losing are too well-timed. I'm not surprised to hear it's all planned. But what does it matter? You knew how I felt, didn't you Nat?

Nat I've always—wished you were a better Watcher.

Tracy And underneath all your belief, wasn't there a grain of doubt? But you took no notice of it. You wanted to believe. You still do. Both of you, so BELIEVE. Like you always did. That's what matters—that's what makes the difference to life.

Nat Yes, but . . .

Tracy You talk about faith, faith in the Team. Well, where's *your* faith? Soon as it's put to the test—away it goes. Brush up your faith, both of you. If you believe in the Game, then the Game goes on, for *you*!

Dawn (*doubtfully*) Do you mean there really is a Bobby Setter-field after all?

Tracy There is for you. If you believe in him.

Dawn Oh, I do. Of course I do. Oh, Bobby I let you down.

Nat (*sententiously*) You must never do that again, Dawn. Faith in the Team. That's what counts. Like your mum says.

Tracy So let's put this back where it belongs. (*She replaces the sweater on the wall*) Now switch on and let's watch the end of the match and forget all this nonsense.

They sit down, Tracy in the middle, facing the screen. Nat switches on. They all sit very still and tense. The noise comes up, with the Commentator's words excited and unintelligible. Tracy sits quietly smiling as Nat and Dawn become reabsorbed in The Game. The Lights dim slowly to Blackout, followed a moment or two later by the fading of the music

FURNITURE AND PROPERTY LIST

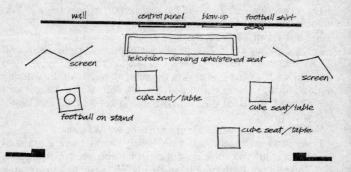

On stage: 2 Screens
Television-viewing seating arrangement
Several cubes used as tables or seats
Football on stand
On wall: control panel with switches and dimmers, blow-up
photograph of footballer, red football shirt

Off stage: Tray with several cans of beer, glasses, packets of cigarettes
and crisps, ashtray, lighter **(Tracy)**
Duster **(Tracy)**
Tray with 2 cups of tea, 2 saucers, 2 teaspoons **(Tracy)**

LIGHTING PLOT

Property fittings required: Strobe light, or rapidly changing colours effect

Interior. A living-room

To open: Normal full lighting

Cue 1	**Nat** turns up sound—second time *Dim general lighting: bring up Strobe and TV screen reflection*	(Page 4)
Cue 2	As **Commentator** announces half-time *Fade TV effect; return to normal lighting*	(Page 5)
Cue 3	**Nat** turns switches *Repeat Cue 1*	(Page 7)

Cue 4	**Commentator** "... by the keeper who clears
	   upfield ..."
	 *Cut TV effect after two or three flashes from
	   Strobe light: bring up normal lighting*
		(Page 7)

Cue 5	**Nat** switches TV on
	 *Bring up TV effect: dim normal lightning. After
	   a few moments gradually fade all lighting to
	   Black-out*
		(Page 11)

EFFECTS PLOT